Cumming

By George Forbes

Lang**Syne**

PUBLISHING

WRITING *to* REMEMBER

Lang**Syne**

PUBLISHING

WRITING *to* REMEMBER

79 Main Street, Newtongrange,
Midlothian EH22 4NA
Tel: 0131 344 0414   Fax: 0845 075 6085
E-mail: info@lang-syne.co.uk
www.langsyneshop.co.uk

Design by Dorothy Meikle
Printed by Ricoh Print Scotland
© Lang Syne Publishers Ltd 2012

ISBN 978-1-85217-098-1

Cumming

SEPT NAMES INCLUDE:

Buchan
Comine
MacNiven
Niven
Russell

Cumming

MOTTO:
Courage.

CREST:
A lion rampant with a dagger in its paw.

TERRITORY:
Roxburghshire, Badenoch and Moray.

Chapter one:

The origins of the clan system

by Rennie McOwan

The original Scottish clans of the Highlands and the great families of the Lowlands and Borders were gatherings of families, relatives, allies and neighbours for mutual protection against rivals or invaders.

Scotland experienced invasion from the Vikings, the Romans and English armies from the south. The Norman invasion of what is now England also had an influence on land-holding in Scotland. Some of these invaders stayed on and in time became 'Scottish'.

The word clan derives from the Gaelic language term 'clann', meaning children, and it was first used many centuries ago as communities were formed around tribal lands in glens and mountain fastnesses.

The format of clans changed over the centuries, but at its best the chief and his family held the land on behalf of all, like trustees, and the ordinary clansmen and women believed they had a blood relationship with the founder of their clan.

There were two way duties and obligations. An inadequate chief could be deposed and replaced by someone of greater ability.

Clan people had an immense pride in race. Their relationship with the chief was like adult children to a father and they had a real dignity.

The concept of clanship is very old and a more feudal notion of authority gradually crept in.

Pictland, for instance, was divided into seven principalities ruled by feudal leaders who were the strongest and most charismatic leaders of their particular groups.

By the sixth century the 'British' kingdoms of Strathclyde, Lothian and Celtic Dalriada (Argyll) had emerged and Scotland, as one nation, began to take shape in the time of King Kenneth MacAlpin.

Some chiefs claimed descent from

ancient kings which may not have been accurate in every case.

By the twelfth and thirteenth centuries the clans and families were more strongly brought under the central control of Scottish monarchs.

Lands were awarded and administered more and more under royal favour, yet the power of the area clan chiefs was still very great.

The long wars to ensure Scotland's independence against the expansionist ideas of English monarchs extended the influence of some clans and reduced the lands of others.

Those who supported Scotland's greatest king, Robert the Bruce, were awarded the territories of the families who had opposed his claim to the Scottish throne.

In the Scottish Borders country – the notorious Debatable Lands – the great families built up a ferocious reputation for providing warlike men accustomed to raiding into England and occasionally fighting one another.

Chiefs had the power to dispense justice

and to confiscate lands and clan warfare produced a society where martial virtues – courage, hardiness, tenacity – were greatly admired.

Gradually the relationship between the clans and the Crown became strained as Scottish monarchs became more orientated to life in the Lowlands and, on occasion, towards England.

The Highland clans spoke a different language, Gaelic, whereas the language of Lowland Scotland and the court was Scots and in more modern times, English.

Highlanders dressed differently, had different customs, and their wild mountain land sometimes seemed almost foreign to people living in the Lowlands.

It must be emphasised that Gaelic culture was very rich and story-telling, poetry, piping, the clarsach (harp) and other music all flourished and were greatly respected.

Highland culture was different from other parts of Scotland but it was not inferior or less sophisticated.

Central Government, whether in London

*"The spirit of the clan means much
to thousands of people"*

or Edinburgh, sometimes saw the Gaelic clans as a challenge to their authority and some sent expeditions into the Highlands and west to crush the power of the Lords of the Isles.

Nevertheless, when the eighteenth century Jacobite Risings came along the cause of the Stuarts was mainly supported by Highland clans.

The word Jacobite comes from the Latin for James – Jacobus. The Jacobites wanted to restore the exiled Stuarts to the throne of Britain.

The monarchies of Scotland and England became one in 1603 when King James VI of Scotland (1st of England) gained the English throne after Queen Elizabeth died.

The Union of Parliaments of Scotland and England, the Treaty of Union, took place in 1707.

Some Highland clans, of course, and Lowland families opposed the Jacobites and supported the incoming Hanoverians.

After the Jacobite cause finally went down at Culloden in 1746 a kind of ethnic cleansing took place. The power of the chiefs was curtailed. Tartan and the pipes were banned in law.

Many emigrated, some because they wanted to, some because they were evicted by force. In addition, many Highlanders left for the cities of the south to seek work.

Many of the clan lands became home to sheep and deer shooting estates.

But the warlike traditions of the clans and the great Lowland and Border families lived on, with their descendants fighting bravely for freedom in two world wars.

Remember the men from whence you came, says the Gaelic proverb, and to that could be added the role of many heroic women.

The spirit of the clan, of having roots, whether Highland or Lowland, means much to thousands of people.

Chapter two:

At the top table

The Cummings clan claim a legendary lineage - direct from the Holy Roman Emperor Charle-magne himself.

The name orginates from Comines near Lisle in northern France on the Flanders frontier with Belgium and is derived from the Comyn family, one of the most powerful factions in medieval Scotland before they were eclipsed by their rivals in the Bruce camp.

Robert de Comyn, a Flemish adventurer, first set foot on the south shore of Britain when he sailed over with the invading Norman forces of William the Conqueror in 1066, eventually securing extensive land holdings in Northumberland, a strategically important area for the Continental conquerors among their northern outposts.

However, some clan historians dispute this version of events, claiming the family name comes from the cumin plant (a variation of wheat).

Others, seeking a purely Scottish heritage, claim they had connections with two abbots of Iona called Comyn who held office in the years 597 and 657.

Another origin of the family is recounted by Wyntoun in his *Cronykil of Scotland*.

According to this medieval scribe, there was at the court of King Malcolm III a young foreign aristocrat whose honorary occupation was Usher of the Royal Apartments (a kind of glorified doorkeeper) and to begin with the only two Scottish words he knew were "come in". Accordingly he became known by that name.

He eventually married the only daughter of the king's half brother Donald Bane and his descendants therefore represented the legitimate line of the ancient Celtic kings.

But to return to the historically proven and more feasible Robert Comyn, who came over with William the Conqueror and who is still the most likely ancestor of the clan, his hold on his Northumberland fiefdom proved tenuous and his feudal underlings soon burned down the house in Durham where he was lodging - with their overlord sealed inside.

The rebelling Northumbrians also slaughtered Robert's 700 soldiers (no mean feat) at their barracks in the city.

William the Conqueror retaliated with typically brutal thoroughness, marching northwards with fire and sword, putting any rebels to death and stringing others up on makeshift gibbets along the main roadways as grim examples.

The murdered Robert's grandson migrated over the border to Scotland in the reign of King David I in the mid-twelfth century and was granted estates in Roxburghshire.

He eventually attained the position of Chancellor of Scotland. These Comyns must have been men of real ability since they were often so swiftly promoted to positions of important authority.

His nephew married into the royal family while a descendant married the Countess of Buchan and his son went on to become Earl of

Menteith and also acquired the Lordship of
Badenoch by a grant of King Alexander II.

Thus the Comyns had a string of titles to
their name, including earldoms and other high
feudal honours, and had a place at the top table
when it came to the wheeling and dealing that was
Scottish politics in those fraught times.

Richard de Comyn stood high in the serv-
ice of William the Lion; while in the days of King
Alexander II the great Comyn Lord of Kilbride
and his wife were the chief movers behind the
construction of Glasgow Cathedral in the mid-
thirteenth century.

When the great work was only half finished, Comyn died. His wife, however, in loving
faithfulness completed the building as a token of
her heartfelt devotion.

There still exists in the lower crypt the
two fine likenesses of the Comyn and his lady
carved in stone alongside a lifelike head of
Alexander II himself; and the three are believed to
be the earliest existing reproductions of historical
personages in Scotland.

A few years later, in the reign of King Alexander III, there were in Scotland, according to the historian Fordun, no fewer than 32 knights called Comyn.

There was also a Comyn Lord of Strathbogie and as Lords of Badenoch they owned the formidable stronghold of Lochindorb in that untamed wilderness as well as a score of huge and important castles throughout the land, from the verdant vales of the Borders to the granite peaks of the North East.

Tales of their chivalric deeds and achievements filled the Scottish annals of their time.

During the boyhood of Alexander III when Henry III of England was doing his best by fraud and force to bring Scotland under his power, it was Walter Comyn, then Earl of Menteith, who stood out as the most patriotic of all the nobles north of the border to resist the threat of English tyranny.

When Henry, at the arranged dynastic marriage of his daughter to the Scots boy-king, suggested that the latter should render fealty for the Kingdom of Scotland, it was Walter Comyn who put the answer into the youngster's mouth - that he "had come into England upon a joyful and pacific errand and would not treat upon so arduous a question without the advice of the Estates of Scotland!"

And when Henry marched towards the Borders at the head of his threatening army, it was Walter Comyn who rallied an opposing Scottish force and made the English modify their territorial ambitions.

But just when he had achieved a period of power and stability, Walter died in mysterious circumstances.

The official version was that he broke his neck after falling from his horse: but the truth seems to have been that an English baron called Russell had become the illicit lover of Comyn's wife and that she was so besotted that she poisoned her husband's bedtime drink.

This pair were eventually driven from their estate and the Earldom later vanished following the debacle with the Bruce faction, eventually being handed over and split up between Stewarts and Grahams.

But two decades before that happened, the nephew of the Earl of Menteith became known as the Red Comyn and his son became the Black Comyn, the latter being one of the six officially appointed guardians of the Maid of Norway following King Alexander III's accidental death after he fell from his horse one night on the rocky shore near Burntisland.

The Comyns were always astute when it came to marrying into prestigious families and the Black Comyn was no exception, marrying Marjory, the sister of John Balliol, a claimant to the throne after the Maid of Norway tragically died from a fever en route by ship to her new realm.

The Black Comyn also put in a claim for the Scottish throne himself since he was a direct descendent of Donald Bane, second son of King Duncan I.

He was not alone in this since there were at least half a dozen other claimants of varying degrees of authenticity when it came to having royal lineage.

The Black Comyn eventually put his support behind Balliol, sheltering him in Badenoch and being imprisoned in the Tower of London for his pains after King John abdicated.

Released to help his cousin, the Earl of Buchan, suppress unrest in Moray in 1297, Comyn instead joined up with William Wallace's patriotic army.

He died in 1303 but his son, also called John though taking the name of 'the Red' to distinguish him from his father, not only continued the family line but also the claim to the throne.

He too ended up in the Tower of London but was among those Scots liberated to join the English King Edward Ist's war in France.

Along with several other noblemen, he broke away to seek French help for Scotland and made his way homeward to join Wallace's forces.

He managed to negotiate a truce with the English in 1304 but there was bad blood between him and Robert the Bruce, to such an extent that Comyn in a heated argument publicly seized his arch enemy by the throat during a meeting of the Scottish Council in Peebles.

Two years later his subsequent confrontation with Robert the Bruce, by that time the leading claimant, at the church of the Greyfriars in Dumfries, a nervous night-time meeting held to hopefully agree a compromise between the two ruthlessly ambitious men, deteriorated into one of the most violent and controversial incidents in Scottish history.

Whether Bruce had not forgotten the earlier clash, whether Comyn threatened to reveal his rival's plans to the English (or in fact had already done so), whether Bruce had all along planned assassination, voices gradually became raised in heated argument, daggers were drawn and Comyn collapsed on the stone floor in front of the altar, bleeding profusely, mortally stabbed by Bruce (though finished off by his servant), an act of sacrilege which led to excommunication from the Pope in Rome.

Comyn's son fled to seek sanctuary with the English and was later killed at Bannockburn.

Always darting in and out of intrigues, one year on top, the next in disgrace, the Comyns had finally met their match in the redoubtable Bruce.

After the Greyfriars murder, their influence dramatically declined and when Bruce became King Robert I he quickly forfeited their estates and stripped them of all their titles and powers, thus ensuring they could never again be the power in the land that they had once been.

Chapter three:

Clan clashes

**Alexander of Argyll had married the Red
Comyn's daughter and for that reason his son,
John of Lorne, became a bitter enemy of
Robert the Bruce, his family's arch foe.**

When Bruce was a fugitive in the heather,
John tried to hunt him down: but when the tables
were eventually turned after Bannockburn it was
payback time and the Lornes duly and wisely
vanished from the scene.

Only a tame sept of the once proud
original family survived as MacDougalls of
Dunolly.

The same obliterating fate overcame most
connected with the great house of Comyn - they
were either put to the sword, fled the country or
their name was subsumed into another clan.

The Comyns of the north were defeated
by Bruce at the battle of Inverurie in
Aberdeenshire in 1308, even though he was being

carried about on a litter because of illness when the clash began.

Pulling himself together with typical fortitude, Bruce mounted his horse and then led his men into victory against their arch enemies. It was said that somehow Bruce miraculously revived not only himself but also the spirits of his whole army whichprevious to this moment had been at a low ebb.

The defeated Comyn fled south (a regular family trait during this harassing time) and his estates were plundered by the jubilant victors. In the churchyard of Bourtie in Aberdeenshire lies the stone effigy of a knight said to have been one of the Comyns slain at the battle of Inverurie.

Gradually throughout the land the Comyns were supplanted by other families.

An instance of this took place on Speyside when a younger son of Grant of Stratherrick eloped with a daughter of a MacGregor chieftain.

Along with 30 followers, the romantic pair fled to Strathspey and found a hiding place in a cavern not far from the castle then known as Freuchie, which was a Comyn stronghold, from which they reigned over the surrounding neighbourhood.

The Comyns looked with disfavour upon such an unwanted intrusion into their traditional lands and tried to dislodge the little band but Grant somehow held out and kept possession of the cave.

Then MacGregor descended along Strathspey at the head of a party of his clan and demanded the return of his daughter.

His defiant son-in-law proved astute. Receiving him with every show of respect, he then somehow contrived in the torchlight and among the shadows of the woodlands to make his men appear a much larger force than they actually were; and a tense reconciliation duly took place.

Grant then pushed his advantage further and complained of attacks from the Comyns, thus inducing MacGregor, always keen on a good scrap, to join in an assault on Freuchie Castle.

By stratagem and sheer guts, they took the stronghold and the chieftain of the Comyns was slain in the brutal attack, his skull remaining a trophy in the possession of the Earl of Seafield to this day.

The Comyns of Dunphail in Moray suffered a similar fate when their old privileges as Wardens of Darnaway royal forest were restricted by the upstart nephew of Bruce, Thomas Randolph.

The Comyns, their honour cut to the quick, set out with a thousand strong force under the leadership of young Alastair of Dunphail to burn Randolph's new great hall at Darnaway.

The force, however, was ambushed at Whitemire and cut to pieces, though young Alastair fought his way through to the River Findhorn where he found the further bank lined by his foes.

Flinging his standard among them with the defiant shout, "Let the bravest keep it!" he then leapt over the river and with four of his followers made good his escape. Randolph then besieged Alastair's father in Dunphail Castle, reducing the garrison to starvation point.

On one dark night, however, Alastair managed to heave some bags of meal from a high bank, using a makeshift wooden catapult cut from trees, over the castle parapets and into the starving stronghold.

The following day, by means of blood-hounds, Alastair was tracked down to his hiding place in a cave beside the Divie River.

He begged to be allowed to die by the sword but was instead smothered by thick smoke after Randolph's troops lit a bonfire at the cave's entrance.

His corpse was then beheaded and the same happened to some of his followers. The decapitated heads were thrown into the courtyard of the castle with the shout, "Here is beef for your bannocks!"

The old chief tearfully held up the head of his son by the hair and declared, "It is indeed a bit-ter morsel - but I will gnaw the last bone of it before I will surrender!"

Eventually, a few days later, the garri-son, driven mad by hunger, charged wildly out of the castle and were cut to pieces by the sur-rounding troops.

In the early nineteenth century, the minister of Edinkilly found the skeletons of Alastair and six of his companions at a spot still known as the Grave of the Headless Comyns.

In succeeding hostilities with the English, King Edward III overran the north of Scotland and made David Comyn the Earl of Atholl and governor of the country.

But, like so much else about the Comyns, it was a very temporary triumph because Bruce's brother-in-law, Sir Andrew Moray, killed David at the battle of Kiblene.

In common with other Highland clans, the Comyns also had centuries long feuds with their neighbours. In particular they had long standing rivalries with the powerful Mackintoshes and tried to drown their foes by raising the waters round their castle stronghold in Loch Moy, an attempt that failed when a Mackintosh clansman set out on a raft one moonless night and broke the dam which resulted in the besieging Comyns being deluged with the floodwaters.

On another occasion the Comyns, pretending peace, invited the Mackintoshes to a feast at Rait Castle near Nairn where, at a secret signal, each Comyn clansman was to stab the rival seated to his left in the heart.

However, a daughter of one of the Comyns was in love with a Mackintosh and revealed the plot, with the result that the Mackintoshes gave their own signal first - and the plotters were duly and fatally hoisted with their own petard.

Another brutal incident arose when Comyn of Badenoch suspected his wife of having an affair with his neighbour, Mackintosh of Tyrnie.

His jealousy reached boiling point when the Mackintosh presented her with a gift of a bull and a dozen cows.

The Mackintoshes were invited to a feast and this time they were all slain.

After the power of the Comyns declined, the Macintoshes and Macphersons moved in on their lands; and on one occasion Alexander Macpherson, known as the Revengeful because of his brutal and ruthless deeds of retaliation, slew nine of the Comyns in a cave where they had been hiding.

Chapter four:

A change of identity

With the decline in their fortunes in the mid-fourteenth century came a change of name; for thereafter the Comyns took the name Cumming as if to dissociate themselves from their failed ancestors.

The main line of the Comyns died out anyway with the death of the Red Comyns last son in 1325.

The Comyns of Altyre became titular chiefs with little real power, certainly not in comparison to their forebears, but one member did marry into the Gordons of Gordonstoun, thus creating the name Gordon-Cumming.

Sir Alexander Cumming of Altyre was created a baronet in 1804 and became an M.P. representing the Dumfries burghs; while the second baronet was a member for the Elgin burghs at the time of the Reform Bill (one son was a famous lion hunter and a daughter was a

renowned travel writer). The fourth baronet, Sir
William Gordon-Cumming of Altyre, served with
the Scots Guards in the Zulu War of 1879 and
later in the Camel Regiment of Egypt during the
pacification of the Nile Delta.

He was also involved in the Royal
Baccarat Scandal in which the Prince of Wales,
later King Edward VII, became the first member
of the royal family to give evidence in a court
action for slander arising from an accusation of
cheating at cards.

This branch of the family kept the
royal connection by acquiring the estate of
Gordounstoun, now better known because of the
public school which educated Prince Philip and
Prince Charles.

Other names derived from Comyn and
variations of Cumming included Cummin,
Cummins, Cumyn, Commyn, Cumine and
Cummine.

Other Comyns, in addition to the Altyre
line, did survive the vengeance of Robert the Bruce.

For example, a branch at Auchmacoy near

Ellon in Aberdeenshire were spared when they vowed allegiance to Bruce and chose the name of Buchan instead of the hated one of Comyn.

Their descendants still occupy the estate at Auchmacoy.

Other former Comyn lines can be found surviving at Culter in Aberdeenshire and Relugas near Forres in Moray.

The major castles associated with the clan were at Dalswinton in Dumfriesshire, Ruthven in Badenoch (now the site of the ruined barracks), Inverlochy in Inverness-shire, Balvenie in Banffshire, Lochindorb in Moray, Bedrule in the Borders, Machan in Perthshire and Kirkintilloch in Dunbartonshire.

They also held lands in Tarset and Tynedale in Northumberland.

This geographic spread shows the powerful range that this family once possessed both in Scotland and over the north of England.